LET'S PRAISE!

Written by Mandy Muir

Illustrated and Designed by Julé Jackson

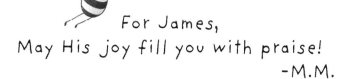

For James,
May His joy fill you with praise!
                              -M.M.

What a Friend we have in Jesus!
                              -J.J.

Hey there!

Have you ever thought about how you can praise God? Come follow along and find out how!

You might think that
you are small.

Look at the sea lions clapping their flippers!

Have you ever seen leaves blowing in the wind?

God gave you breath to praise Him!

BLOW the leaves higher and higher. Good job!

Birds love to sing praises to God.

You can even praise God when you eat and drink.

Frogs use their hands and feet to make flying leaps!

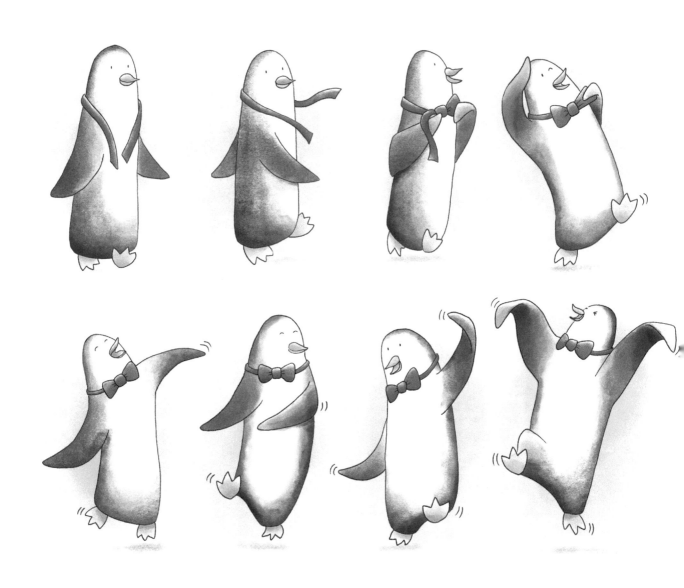

A penguin's walk kind of looks like a dance.

Can you find the praying mantis?

PRAYING is a way you talk to God and praise Him.

Fill in the blank:
God, I praise You for _____!

Now you know MANY WAYS that you can praise God.

RAISE your hands way up high

CLAP

CLAP

CLAP

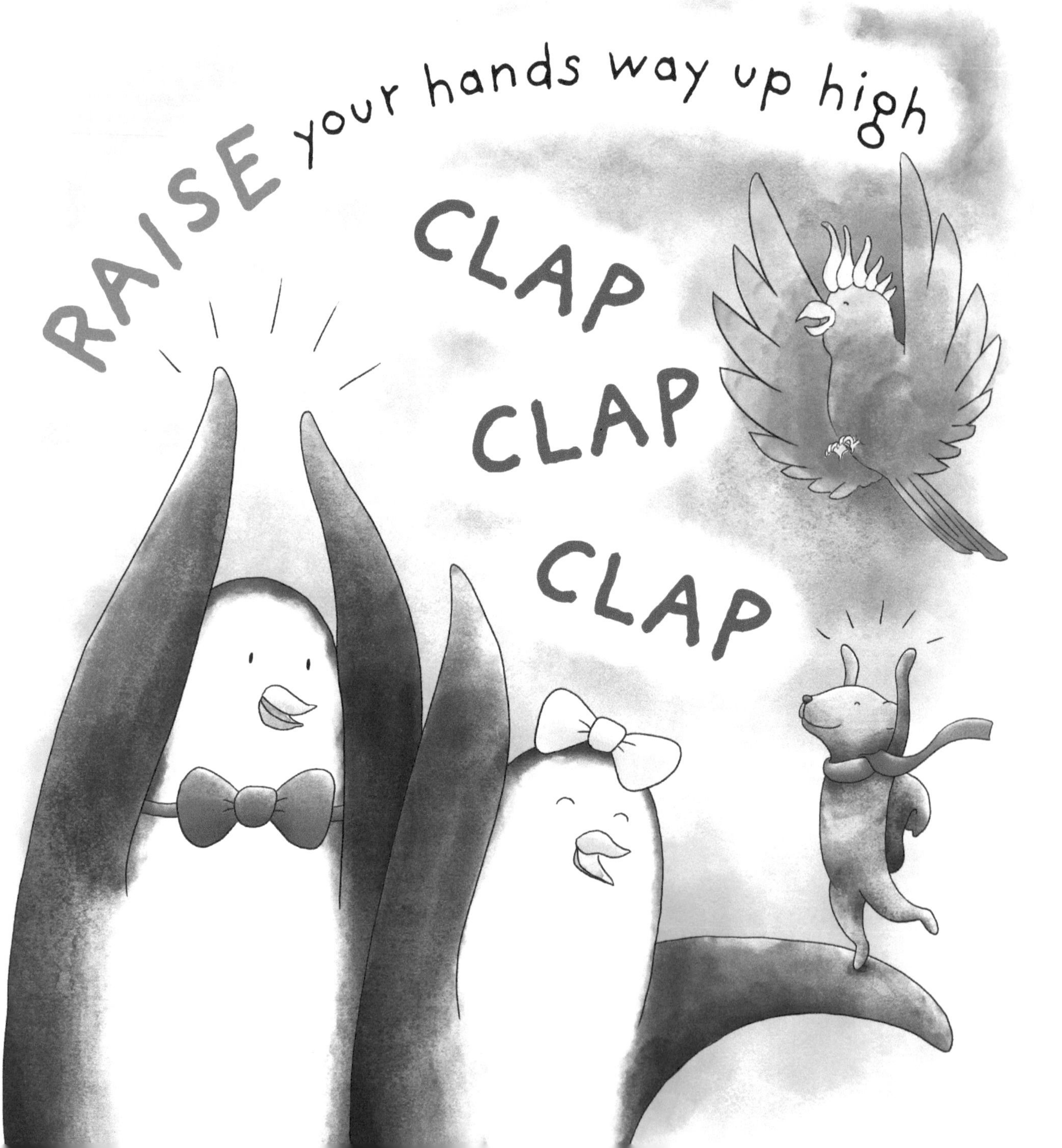

Take a deep breath and **BLOW**

SING LA LA LA

SHAKE to the left

SHAKE to the right

God, we praise You most of all for YESUS!

Let everything that has breath praise the Lord! Praise the Lord!
Psalm 150:6

Printed in the USA
CPSIA information can be obtained
at www.ICGtesting.com
LVHW071751011123
762562LV00020B/798